You Can Tell It's Hunting Season...

A Shot at Humor Aimin' to Make You Laugh!

Inspired by Faith

You Can Tell It's Hunting Season...
ISBN 978-0-9848369-8-7

Published by Product Concept Mfg., Inc.
2175 N. Academy Circle #200, Colorado Springs, CO 80909

©2012 Product Concept Mfg., Inc. All rights reserved.

Written and Compiled by Patricia Mitchell
in association with Product Concept Mfg., Inc.

Sayings not having a credit listed are contributed by writers
for Product Concept Mfg., Inc. or in a rare case,
the author is unknown.

You Can Tell It's Hunting Season...

When do duck hunters wake up?
At the quack of dawn!

Adventure and pleasure—plus the company of like-minded folks who relish trudging across a winter-crisp field and hunkering down in a well-hidden blind in wait for that one perfect moment. What's not to like? And as any hunter knows, the thrill doesn't close with the season, but continues in stories, memories, and friendships made to last a lifetime.

You Can Tell It's Hunting Season is a collection of cartoons and quips, jokes and anecdotes hunters can relate to. Hunters who know how to laugh at themselves will get a chuckle out of their sport from the point of view of wild game. Any hunter who has ever felt outshone by his hound will nod in recognition at the super-clever canines and their hapless owners. And non-hunters? Perhaps they'll better identify with the cat who would rather spend the glorious hours curled up in a warm, dry cabin!

Whether you're sitting by the campfire after a great day or relaxing at home between seasons, let *Hunting Season* tickle your funny bone and spark your own humorous hunting stories. We aim to make you laugh out loud!

You know you're
a hunter if:

The phrase "'Tis the season" means Hunting Season.

Your idea of home décor includes antlers.

It's too cold to shovel snow, but lying in it for hours waiting for geese to fly is a great adventure.

Your bird dog is your best friend.

You wonder why anyone would go on a summer vacation.

You have the location of your deer stand saved on your GPS.

Someone in a crowd yells "Duck!" and you reach for your gun.

It took you five weekends to put up the kids' tree house, but you can hang a dozen deer stands in a day.

"Shooting the bull" isn't just an expression.

Your favorite book is the sportsman's catalog.

One Sunday a minister feigned illness so he could go out hunting. That very morning, he shot a trophy-sized deer with an elegant dense 14-point rack. Saint Peter, looking down from heaven, said to God, "You aren't going to let him bag a prize like that, are You?"

"Why not?" God replied. "Who's he going to tell?"

Man, look at the size of those tracks!
Lemme go see where he came from, and you go see where he went.

Then there's the hunter who found himself cornered by a ferocious lion. Seeing no escape, the hunter fell on his knees in prayer. To his astonishment, he saw the lion doing the same thing.

"God has worked a miracle!" cried the hunter, much relieved. "A ferocious beast is joining me in prayer!"

"Hush," admonished the lion. "I'm saying grace."

On his way home from the hunt, this hunter stops at the grocery store and goes to the meat counter. "Gimme a couple of ducks," he says to the butcher.

"Sorry, all sold out," the butcher says, "but I've got some chickens left. Those be okay?"

"Chickens!" the hunter cries in dismay. "How can I go home and tell my wife I bagged a couple of chickens?"

Did you hear the one about:

The hunter who lost his dog in the forest? So he put his ear up to a tree and listened for a bark.

The hunter who came home with a 25-pound turkey? He had his wife convinced until she noticed the Butcher's stamp.

The hunter and his camouflage jacket? No matter how hard he looked for it, he couldn't find it!

The hunter who came across a deer that had an upset stomach? He shot him with Elk-a-Seltzer.

The moose that walked into a diner? "We don't serve moose," the waitress told him. "That's OK," the moose replied. "A cup of coffee will do me."

The hunter who took up skeet shooting, then stopped? He didn't like the way they tasted.

The hunter who went to get a closer look at some tracks? That's when he got hit by a train.

"God meant for us to hunt!" a hunter claimed to his skeptical friend.

"How do you know that?" he asked in reply.

"Because if He hadn't," the hunter said, "God wouldn't have given us thermal socks and plaid shirts!"

You can always tell the difference
between a hunter and a fisherman.
The hunter lies in wait.
The fisherman waits and lies.

A hunter, who had a dog
that could walk on water,
was determined to impress
a friend, who always saw
the down side of anything.
So he took his friend and
his dog out duck hunting.
Sitting at the lake's edge, the
hunter soon downed a duck,
and his dog trotted across
the water, retrieved the duck,
and brought it back to his
master. "Humph!" snorted
his friend. "So yer dog don't
know how to swim?"

Two hunters were walking in the forest when they were suddenly confronted by a mean-tempered grizzly bear. One hunter turned and ran. His companion yelled after him: "Don't you know you can't outrun a grizzly bear?"

"I don't need to outrun the bear," he hollered back. "I only need to outrun you!"

Two hunters were boasting about their clever bird dogs. "My dog's so good," one proclaimed, "that he knows where the turkey's going to land before I even shoot it!"

"Yeah, I know," replied the other.

"So how'd you know?" the bragger asked.

"My dog told me."

Willy's Little Bits O' Wisdom

A bird in the hand…
is why a hunter sits
in a blind all day.

Two hunters meet each other in the forest. "Hey, am I ever glad to see you!" says one. "I've been lost for hours!"

"That's nothing," replies the other. "I've been lost for a week."

WORK IS FOR PEOPLE
WHO DON'T KNOW
HOW TO HUNT.

Hunters prefer dogs because...

Unlike your fashion-challenged retriever, no cat would suffer the embarrassment of being seen wearing a bright orange neoprene vest.

If you take a cat duck hunting, she's more interested in your spinning wing decoys than in the real thing.

You and your dog can tromp through the mud; fine. The cat will clean herself at the mere mention of mud.

There's no way a cat is going to crouch down on the ground with you. She might, however, curl up on your lap, in which case you should not move, because it would disturb her nap.

Your dog perks up at the sound of gunshot; a cat darts to the nearest hiding place and refuses to come out for the rest of the day.

Your dog watches your every move. A cat couldn't care less.

At dusk, the dog says, "Awww shucks...is it really time to go home already?" The cat, without saying a thing, has left a long time ago.

A quail got caught in the line of sight between two hunters, and they opened fire on him. Miraculously, the bird escaped, but when he returned to his mate, she saw that his feathers were in extreme disarray, and he was clearly distraught.

"Oh, dear!" she cried in dismay. "Did you get shot at?"

"Yes, I certainly did," her mate replied, "but the hunters missed me. In getting away from them, however, I was flying so low over the park that I got caught between two people playing badminton."

**Bob mistakenly blew his buck call
instead of his duck call.**

And I'm tellin' ya, buddy, he was huge!

There's the story of an old farmer who had a mule for sale. "She'll point quail better than any bird dog," he told a hunter who came to look at her. Impressed, the hunter bought her and decided to ride her home.

On the way home, he had to cross a river. All went well until halfway across the river, when the mule squatted down, thoroughly soaking her rider. Furious, the hunter took her back to the farmer and complained.

"Forgot to tell you," the farmer told him, "she's such an amazing mule that she points fish, too."

Wanda's Little Bits O' Wisdom

Early to bed, early to rise...
it must be hunting season!

Of course you're tuckered out.
You know, in dog years,
you're 250 years old!

Two hunters hired a pilot to fly them far into the wilderness for deer hunting. When the pilot returned to take them back to the city, he saw they had bagged six bucks. "Plane won't carry the weight of six," the pilot informed them. "You'll have to leave two of those bucks here."

Unwilling to leave their prize specimens behind, the hunters protested. "But we loaded six last year in a plane exactly this size!" The pilot gave in and let the hunters pull the bucks aboard, and they all took off. Five minutes later the plane crashed into the dense forest.

"Any idea where we are?" asked one of the hunters.

"Yep," his pal replied. "Right about where we went down last year."

A taciturn man and a woman were on their first date. The woman, trying to open a conversation that would interest him, said, "I hear that you hunt bear."

"Nope," replied the man. "I'm fully clothed when I hunt."

Willy's Little Bits O' Wisdom

A place for everything...
isn't available in a
duck blind.

"My bird dog has more brains than most people," Jones boasted. When his hunting friends hooted and guffawed, Jones told his story:

"Last year, our house caught fire. In our panic, my wife and I ran around grabbing clothes, electronics, dishes, pictures— you name it, whatever we could manage to drag out of that house, we did. When the smoke got so thick we couldn't go back inside, that's when I saw my dog run in. He bounded out a few minutes later with something in his mouth. Boys, it was our insurance policy."

What do you get
when you cross a
telephone with a
hunting dog?
A golden receiver!

How can lost hunters
find their way
in the woods?
**By listening to the
tree bark!**

What grows up and
grows down at the
same time?
Geese.

Two hunters were scouting out the territory when they came to a sign reading, BEWARE OF BEARS. "No problem," said one hunter, "because I'm carrying my lucky charm." With that, he drew out of his pocket a rabbit's foot. "Wear this," the hunter continued, "and it keeps the bears away."

"Hmmm," his friend replied skeptically. "Might work—depending on how fast you can run."

A hunter bought two bird dogs, but after he got them home, he realized he couldn't tell them apart. When he told a friend about his problem, the friend suggested he measure them. "Great idea!" the hunter said.

So he went home and measured the two dogs. "Sure 'nuff," the hunter reported back to his friend. "The one with brown spots is a full two inches taller than the one with tan spots!"

**A steady job has ruined
many a good hunter.**

Two hunters woke up in the middle of the night. "Look at the stars!" one rhapsodized. "What splendor! What a magnificent example of God's creation!"

Far less enthusiastically, the other replied, "Yeah. But what do you think happened to our tent?"

Willy's Little Bits O' Wisdom

So many deer,
so few sick days.

A first-time hunter had taken aim and was just about to fire when his experienced partner stopped him.

"Why'd you do that?" the novice exclaimed. "I distinctly heard that moose moo!"

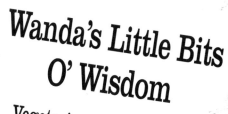

Wanda's Little Bits O' Wisdom

Vegetarian: Politically correct term for someone who doesn't know how to hunt.

A hunter who was an atheist was out in the woods when suddenly a 2,000-pound bear jumps out at him.

"Oh my God," he yelled, "help!"

A voice from heaven spoke. "Why are you asking me for help? I thought you didn't believe in Me."

"Before right now, I didn't believe in 2,000-pound bears, either!"

A bachelor hunter had recently bought two new pointers, and he invited his mother over to take a look at them and join him for dinner. After admiring the dogs, she sat down at the dining room table, and her son brought in the food. She noticed the dishes were crusted with food, and asked politely, "Do you use soap and water when you do dishes, dear?"

"Sure, Mom," her son replied. Despite her misgivings, Mom enjoyed the meal and praised her son's cooking skills.

"Thanks, Mom," he said as he spread out the plate on the floor, whistled and called, "here, Soap! Here, Water!"

Two lion hunters rented a cabin. The next morning, one got up early to begin the hunt. Soon he spotted a lion, aimed, and fired, but the bullet only grazed its coat. Enraged, the beast turned on the hunter, who ran as fast as he could back to the cabin. Just as he reached the cabin, however, he tripped, and the lion fell headlong into him, both man and animal tumbling into the cabin. "What a catch!" his pal exclaimed as he grabbed his gun, ran outside, and slammed the door shut after him. "You take care of this one while I go bag one myself!"

If you're a bear...

You get to sleep for six months at a time.

You can eat all you want and gain all you want while you're awake, because you'll lose it while you sleep.

You never have to shave.

You stand up, and everyone takes you seriously.

You get to growl all you want. In fact, you're expected to growl!

Willy's Little Bits O' Wisdom

Fire up the grill!

Hunters don't catch and release.

Two geese were flying over
the lake when a fighter jet,
its jetstream flaring behind it,
zoomed above them. "Wow,"
said one admiringly. "I sure wish
I could fly like that!"

"And you would, too," the other
said, "if *your* tail were on fire!"

A hunter had a dog so smart that he knew what to hunt just by the kind of gun his owner carried. When he saw the rifle, the dog chased deer without a glance at any other game. When he saw the shotgun, he faithfully pointed quail; and when he saw the squirrel rifle, he single-mindedly treed squirrels.

One Christmas, the hunter's wife bought her husband a new 5-iron. When he held it up to examine it, the smart dog sprang to his feet and immediately fetched a golf ball.

"Look," shouted one skunk to his chum, "there's that hunter over there, and I think he's aiming right at us!"

His chum calmly bowed and said, "Let us spray."

There's the old story of a hunter who had the best bird dog in the country. The dog could sniff out any kind of bird and hold point on it for as long as necessary.

One day, after a successful day of hunting, the hunter and his dog were sitting by the campfire when another hunter approached them. Suddenly, the bird dog sprang to attention and went into point at the stranger. Perplexed at his dog's behavior, the hunter asked the man, "Are you carrying a bird?"

"No," the man replied. "Got nothing all day."

"Well," the hunter said, "I'm sorry my dog is acting this way, and I do apologize. Please, won't you join us?"

As he sat down, he proceeded to introduce himself: "Name's Partridge. Yours?"

A ranger, instructing a group of new hunters, was offering safety tips. "Never," intoned the ranger, "run away from a bear."

One hand flew up. "How come?"

"Because it might be a bear that likes fast food," came a voice from the back of the room.

Early to bed.
Early to rise.
Hunt all day.
Make up lies.

What do you call...

A grizzly with no teeth?
A gummy bear.

A frozen Thanksgiving
meal?
A turrrrrrkey.

A duck flying upside down?
Quackers.

A birddog with a
receding hairline?
Bald Spot.

A hunter got lost in the woods and was without food for days. Finally he spied a bald eagle, shot it, and ate it. But right at that moment, a game warden showed up and cited the hunter for killing an endangered species.

When the hunter was brought before the judge, he explained that he thought he would starve to death if he did not eat the bird. The judge dismissed the charge, but then asked the hunter, "I'm curious—exactly what does bald eagle taste like?"

"Oh," the hunter replied, "something close to whooping crane and spotted owl."

Wanda's Little Bits O' Wisdom

A stitch in time...
prevents leaky wading boots.

What should you do if someone
throws a goose at you?
Duck!

What do you say if someone
throws a duck at another duck?
Duck, duck!

What do you say if someone
throws a goose at a duck?
Duck, duck—goose!

On the first day of hunting season, a hunter fell out of his deer stand and broke both his legs. He moaned to the doctor, "Why didn't this happen on my last day of hunting?"

"It did," the doctor replied.

Where did the young hunting dog sleep on his first night out in the field?

In a pup tent!

"Yep, he's a good retriever," one hunter said of his dog. "The season's just opened, and already he's retrieved a couple of hot dogs from someone's campsite."

Ammo? What ammo?
I thought you were bringing the ammo!

Hunters prefer dogs because...

Your dog is as keen as you are to get an early start. A cat will sleep until she's good and ready to get up, which might be around noon.

Your dog is willing to jump in a cold lake, retrieve a duck, and bring it back to you. No amount of cajoling will convince a cat to do the same thing.

Your dog obeys your orders; a cat glances at you and walks away.

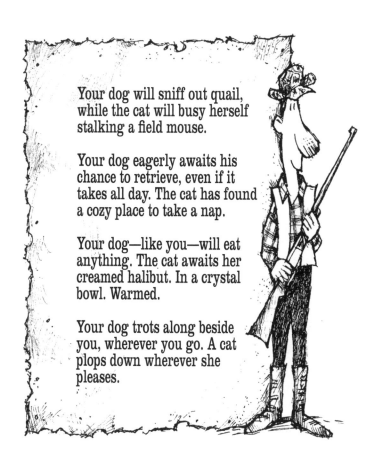

Your dog will sniff out quail, while the cat will busy herself stalking a field mouse.

Your dog eagerly awaits his chance to retrieve, even if it takes all day. The cat has found a cozy place to take a nap.

Your dog—like you—will eat anything. The cat awaits her creamed halibut. In a crystal bowl. Warmed.

Your dog trots along beside you, wherever you go. A cat plops down wherever she pleases.

Two rabbits were running away from a couple of hounds. "Hey!" one rabbit shouted to the other after they had put some distance between themselves and the hounds. "Let's just stop a spell, and before those dogs get here, we'll outnumber them!"

A hunter decided to take his wife out hunting, hoping to impress her with his skill. Soon, a skein of ducks flew over, and with three shots from the hunter's gun, three ducks came down.

"Pretty good, huh, honey?" the hunter gloated as his dog retrieved the birds.

"Well, I guess so," his wife replied with some hesitation. "But it seems to me hitting the water from so high would have killed them anyway."

How come...

You spring up at dawn for the weekend hunt, but can't wake up before noon on any other Saturday?

You feel great up in the tree stand, but get dizzy standing on a ladder to paint the ceiling?

Your dog hates it if you blow in his face, but loves it when he can ride with his head sticking out the window?

Three city slickers decided they'd go hunting. They outfitted themselves in grand style, and then drove out to the country, where it had been snowing. They got out of the car, got their gear, and headed into the woods. Right away, they came across a line of tracks. The first hunter exclaimed, "Look! Deer tracks!"

"No, those aren't deer tracks," the second hunter said knowingly. "Those are squirrel tracks."

"I can tell you they're not squirrel tracks," the third hunter argued. "They're rabbit tracks, for sure."

While all three were arguing, a train came along and hit them.

Ten Reasons Why Most Women Don't Want to Go Hunting

1. There's no place to plug in a hair dryer.

2. You can't carry on a meaningful conversation in a deer blind.

3. Why wouldn't an elk make a good pet?

4. It's far easier to buy poultry from the butcher than to sit for hours in a freezing blind.

5. Ummm...don't those look like bear tracks?

6. There's no room in a duck blind for toiletries, several pairs of shoes, and five changes of clothes.

7. Bright orange is a difficult color to wear; besides, it's rarely in fashion.

8. When a hot, sudsy bubble bath would be most welcome at the end of a grueling day, there's no plumbing within ten miles.

9. Snakes. 'Nuff said.

10. It's just too early to get up!

How do you catch a unique rabbit?
Easy—unique up on it!

How do you catch a tame rabbit?
Tame way—unique up on it!

Wanda's Little Bits O' Wisdom

To hunt or not to hunt...
is a no-brainer.

Did you hear the one about...

The duck that walked into a drugstore? He said to the pharmacist, "Get me some lip balm, and put it on my bill."

The birddog that lost his tail? That's why he went to the retail store.

The hunting dog that ran in circles? He found it difficult to run in squares.

How many hunting dogs does it take to change a light bulb?

Pointer: I see it, I see it! Lemme at it!

Terrier: It isn't running, so who cares?

German Shepherd: Just as soon as I finish patrolling the yard, I'll come in and get right to the light bulb.

Border Collie: Let's get everyone together before we start worrying about a light bulb.

Golden Retriever: Hey, loosen up! The day is young, the sun is shining, so let's not stay indoors worrying about a stupid old light bulb!

Lab: Oh, me, me, me! Pleeeze let me change the light bulb! Can I, huh? Huh?

Hunters were sitting around the campfire reminiscing. "My partners and I were sleeping under the stars," one hunter said, "when a couple grizzlies came around. The other guys jumped out of their sleeping bags and took off like a shot. But me, I was stuck, because my sleeping bag zipper jammed right then!"

"So what'd you do?" queried the other hunters.

"I discovered that it's possible to climb a tree in your sleeping bag."

Things you'll never hear a hunter say...

Got enough ammo, thanks.

Yep, that's all the decoys I need this time.

I think I'll sleep in—go on out without me.

Got to hand it to you, pal—that dog of yours just might be a tad smarter than mine.

I don't have room for that 14-point rack of antlers on my wall.

Camp coffee? Best I ever tasted!

Little too muddy out here for me.
I'm headin' back to the cabin.

Nah, I don't need a bigger blind
bag—all the junk food I need fits
in this one.

I'm not interested in hunting this
weekend—my wife has tickets to
the opera.

I've got a couple regulations
I want to suggest to the game
warden.

"This dog's gone soft," the hunter complained to his wife. "He won't stay on point, gets distracted by any little noise, and would just as soon stay at camp rather than retrieve anything."

"Oh, I don't know about that," said his wife as the dog trotted over with her bunny slippers in his mouth.

The novice hunter goes out into the woods, and in a distance, he spots game. So he shoots. Quite pleased with himself and already formulating the tale he'll tell his buddies, he strides over to tag the animal. Unfortunately, it's lying on the other side of a fence, and a farmer is standing over it.

"That's my moose!" the hunter claims excitedly. "Don't you dare try to take it, or I'll shoot!"

"Sure, sure," says the farmer. "Calm down, pal. All I want to do is get my saddle off it."

Two hunters new to the sport were out hunting. They decided to separate to get a better chance of catching something. The first redneck says to the other, "If you get lost, fire three shots into the air every hour. That way I can pinpoint you and find you." After about three hours, the second redneck finds he is really lost. He decides to fire three shots into the air as the first man told him. He then waits an hour and does it again. He repeats this until he is out of ammo. The next morning, the first redneck finds the second with the help of forest rangers. He asks the second redneck man if he did what he told him to do. The redneck answers, "Yes, I fired three shots into the air every hour on the hour until I ran out of arrows."

Willy's Little Bits O' Wisdom

After all is said and done...
there's more
said than done.

Two turkey hunters, one an optimist and one a pessimist, were returning to camp with their limit in tow. "You have to admit it's been a great day!" the optimist exclaimed. "Perfect weather, invigorating hunt, and we got beautiful birds to take home."

"It was nice," admitted the pessimist, "but it could have been better."

"How?"

"They could have come with dressing, mashed potatoes, and pumpkin pie."

There oughta be a way...

To harness the power produced by a lake full of spinning wing duck decoys.

To guarantee that the first-time hunter who goes along with you doesn't outshoot you.

To make sure no one ever finds out how much you spent on your new duck call.

HUNTING ESSENTIALS

Dozen jelly donuts

2 pkgs. cinnamon rolls

5 bags chips

2 tubs guacamole

6 ham sandwiches

3 gallons strong hot coffee

An elk walked into the lodge restaurant and ordered a hamburger and soda. After he had eaten and was paying the bill, the cashier remarked, "We don't see too many elk come in here."

"At these prices," replied the elk, "I'm not surprised."

Then there was the hunter who asked his minister if it's a sin to hunt on Sundays. "From what I've heard about your aim," the minister replied, "it's a sin for you to hunt at any time."

Willy's Little Bits O' Wisdom

The early bird gets the worm, but the second mouse gets the cheese.

A hunter was driving along a country lane when he came across a sign saying, "Talking bird dog for sale." Intrigued, he stopped the car, walked to the back of the house, and there he saw a black lab resting under the shade of a tree.

"Do you talk?" the hunter asked.

"Sure do," the dog replied.

"And you're a good birder, too?"

"I sure am," said the dog as he rose to his feet. "Been hunting for five years, and I've never loused up a point in my life. Why, before a bird hits the ground, I'm there to pick it up and bring it back. I lay it out right at your feet, and if you want me to,

I'll clean it and get it going on the grill for you."

Highly impressed, the hunter went to the house to find out how much the dog's owner was asking for the dog.

"Ten dollars," the owner said.

"Ten dollars!" gasped the hunter. "Why so little for such a remarkable animal?"

"I'll tell you why," said the owner. "It's because he's a liar. He didn't do half the stuff he was out there telling you about."

Wanda's Little Bits O' Wisdom

If it walks like a duck,
quacks like a duck,
looks like a duck,
it must be a duck.

An old hunter was boasting about the fine raccoon his dog had treed the night before. "I bagged the biggest raccoon I've ever seen—sleek hide as pretty as can be, and enough meat to see us through the whole month."

While he was talking, the game warden showed up and fined him for hunting out of season.

"Two hundred dollars!" the hunter exclaimed when he saw the citation. "And all for a mangy, skinny, tough old raccoon not much bigger than a squirrel!"

There's no point in driving 300 miles to hunt when you can be just as unsuccessful much closer to home.

How ducks know when to fly south.

His faithful hunting dog, Sam, was slowing down, so his owner took him to the vet to get him checked out. A look at the scales quickly revealed the problem: Sam was seriously overweight. The vet handed Sam's owner a bottle of pills, along with instructions to add one pill every day to the dog's food, and then come back in three weeks.

Yet three weeks later, Sam still has not lost weight. "Are you having trouble getting Sam to eat the food you've put the pill in?" asked the vet.

"Not at all," replied Sam's owner. "I always hide it in one of his jelly donuts."

What Non-Hunters Want to Know

Why aren't trails paved so hunters can avoid the mud?

At what age do deer become elk?

Why aren't there places to eat out in the fields?

Are the bears tame?

Why doesn't someone spray the woods so there aren't so many mosquitoes?

Who feeds the ducks?

Why doesn't someone do
something about snakes?

Do stripes make a squirrel
a chipmunk?

Is there any way to get
turkeys to stand still for you?

Is there an app for this?

In the Words of Hunters...

"If there's a fire in your belly, there mighta been too many beans in your chili."

"If somethin' makes your dog's hackles go up, it's no time to be lettin' your guard down."

"Good friends, a good dog, and the good Lord by your side...that's the huntin' life at its best."

Wanda's Little Bits O' Wisdom

There's a fine line between hunting and sitting there looking stupid!

More times than he could count, the hunter messed up the hunt. He would spot a buck, aim, fire, and miss; he would sneeze right when the buck got close, sending it bounding away; he would doze on the stand, waking only to watch two prize bucks scampering off, bushes rustling in their wake.

Frustrated, he complained to his buddies, "Everything that happens to guys who have no idea how to hunt keeps happening to me!"

A duck hunter was pleased that
his wife expressed an interest
in going hunting with him,
so he invited her along on the
next hunt. While they huddled
together in the blind, he showed
her what to do when the duck
started flying.

Soon, he saw a flock headed
their way, and he said excitedly,
"Get ready, honey—grab your

gun!" But instead, he heard a piercing shriek and saw his wife lunge out of the blind.

"What's wrong?" he shouted, "all I said was 'grab your gun'!"

"I did," she screamed back. "But it started slithering away!"

A storm swept through the area, leaving highways, roads, and bridges scattered with debris, downed lines, and stalled cars. Two hunters, however, were determined to get to the woods for the first day of the season, and they got in their truck and started out.

After hours on the road, they were finally halted by a large bulldozer blocking both lanes. A worker climbed out of the machine and yelled, "The road's closed! Didn't you see those cones, traffic barrels, and warning signs back there?"

"Yep, we saw 'em," the driver proudly yelled back to the worker, "and we got by 'em all! Now the only thing that's in our way is your tractor."

Ned's new pup seemed to lack
the essential qualities of a birddog.

Two novice hunters went out duck hunting. They spent all day in the blind, but managed to down nary a bird. At the end of the day, one says to the other, "Ya know, maybe tomorrow we'll catch one by throwing the dog up higher."

A hunter wondered what his dog would do if he were injured while they were on a hunt. To find out, the hunter feigned illness in the blind by lying on the ground and groaning in pain. His dog trotted over, sniffed his owner, then headed straight to his blind bag and gobbled the sandwiches the hunter had packed for lunch.

Get ready for hunting season!

Stand in a tub of frigid water for a couple hours.

Dig up your backyard, and then walk through the mud.

Climb the nearest utility pole, and hold there for a couple hours.

Lie down in the grass and hope your neighbor, the psychiatrist, doesn't see you.

Two hunters were walking across the field when one noticed his buddy's large thermos. "That's sure a big thermos you've got there," he said. His buddy nodded and said, "Yep. Got it yesterday, and the guy told me it's good for keeping hot things hot and cold things cold."

"So what do you have in it?" the first hunter asked.

"Hot coffee and ice tea."

A particularly devout hunter always took his Bible with him so he could read it at the end of the day. One evening, however, he realized he had lost it someplace in the field. The next morning, he searched for the book, but gave up, realizing it could be anywhere.

Later in the day, while he was sitting in his blind, a rabbit approached him with the Bible. Astonished and delighted, the hunter exclaimed, "Praise God! It's a miracle!"

"Not really," the rabbit said as he laid down the Bible. "You had your name in it."

Willy's Little Bits O' Wisdom

Birds of a feather...
are what it's
all about.

The hunter's wife chided her husband for telling her about the same hunting exploit over and over again. He reminded her that she often told the same story many times.

"Not so," she said. "I merely re-share. You repeat."

Which side of a pheasant has the most feathers?

The outside, of course!

When a rabbit and a duck go to dinner, who pays?

The duck, naturally—he always has the bill!

Wanda's Little Bits O' Wisdom

A man who can smile when
things go wrong...
is a hunter who thinks
no one's watching.

A friend asked a hunter about his handsome new dog. "Setter or pointer?"

"Neither," the hunter replied unhappily. "He's a keen upsetter and a great disappointer."

A Hunter's Prayer

I love to hunt, dear God—that's me!
I greet each season eagerly,
And on that first cool autumn day,
I'm up at dawn and on my way—

I'll tramp through fields to find a spot
Where I can take that perfect shot.
From any kind of hidden blind,
The pleasure of the hunt is mine—

Though I may hit, or I may miss,
It's outright fun and utter bliss—
There's just one thing I'd ask, dear God—
Please keep me smarter than my dog!